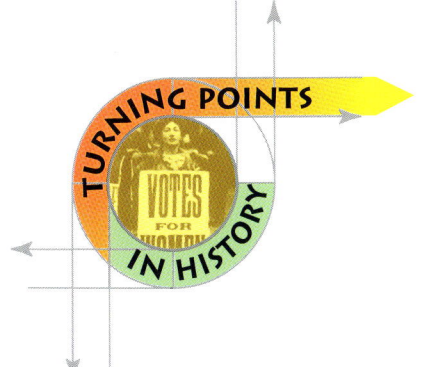

Votes for Women

The Franchise in Britain

STEWART ROSS

Heinemann
LIBRARY

www.heinemann.co.uk/library
Visit our website to find out more information about Heinemann Library books.

To order:
 Phone 44 (0) 1865 888066
 Send a fax to 44 (0) 1865 314091
 Visit the Heinemann Bookshop at www.heinemann.co.uk/library to browse our catalogue and order online.

First published in Great Britain by Heinemann Library, Halley Court, Jordan Hill, Oxford OX2 8EJ, a division of Reed Educational and Professional Publishing Ltd. Heinemann is a registered trademark of Reed Educational & Professional Publishing Ltd.

OXFORD MELBOURNE AUCKLAND JOHANNESBURG BLANTYRE
GABORONE IBADAN PORTSMOUTH NH (USA) CHICAGO

© Reed Educational and Professional Publishing Ltd 2002
The moral right of the proprietor has been asserted.

Produced for Heinemann Library by Discovery Books Limited
Designed by Keith Williams
Originated by Ambassador Litho Limited
Printed in Hong Kong

06 05 04 03
10 9 8 7 6 5 4 3 2

06 05 04 03
10 9 8 7 6 5 4 3 2 1

ISBN 0 431 06940 9 (hardback)

ISBN 0 431 06721 X (paperback)

British Library Cataloguing in Publication Data

Ross, Stewart
Votes for women: the franchise in Britain. - (Turning points in history)
1. Women - Suffrage - Great Britain - Juvenile literature
I. Title
324.6'23'0941

Acknowledgements

The Publishers would like to thank the following for permission to reproduce photographs:
Mary Evans, pp. 4, 5, 7, 9, 12, 21, 22; *Hulton Archive*, pp. 10, 16, 23; *Hulton Deutsch Collection*, pp. 6, 11, 18; *Hulton Getty*, pp. 8, 13, 14, 17, 20, 24, 25; *Peter Newark's Pictures*, pp. 15, 19; *Popperfoto*, pp. 26, 28; *Popperfoto/Reuters*, pp. 27, 29.

Cover photographs reproduced with permission of: (top) *Hulton Deutsch Collection*, (bottom) *Hulton Getty*.

Every effort has been made to contact copyright holders of any material reproduced in this book. Any omissions will be rectified in subsequent printings if notice is given to the Publisher.

Contents

Any words appearing in the text in bold, **like this**, are explained in the Glossary.

The right to vote

Death at the Derby

Epsom Race Course, 1913. Huge crowds were pressing against the rails, straining to see the Derby racehorses thundering towards them. Suddenly, a young woman wrapped in a banner ducked under the rails and ran onto the course. Trying to grab the reins of a horse owned by the king, she was brushed aside and fell to the ground. Her skull was fractured by flying hooves. She died shortly afterwards without regaining consciousness.

DAILY SKETCH.

HISTORY'S MOST WONDERFUL DERBY: FIRST HORSE DISQUALIFIED: A 100 TO 1 CHANCE WINS: SUFFRAGETTE NEARLY KILLED BY THE KING'S COLT.

The front page of the *Daily Sketch* the day after Emily Davison had been fatally injured by the king's horse in the Derby. Despite this terrible accident, the paper still described the race as 'most wonderful'.

The martyr

The young woman was Emily Davison. She was a 'suffragette,' the name given to women who campaigned for the right to vote in parliamentary elections. Emily believed that gaining this right would lead to women having much greater equality with men.

Emily's action certainly attracted attention. Her supporters said she was a martyr. However, the majority of people thought she was crazy and believed she had set back the women's cause.

The turning point

In 1913, about three-fifths of all adult men (some eight million), but no women, had the parliamentary vote. Women had campaigned for many years to have the same voting rights as men, but their demands were always turned down by **Parliament**. The turning point came five years after Emily's death.

The 1918 Representation of the People **Act** gave the vote to 95 per cent of men over 21, and to most women over 30. Ten years later women were finally given the vote on the same terms as men.

On 18 June 1910, there was a so-called 'Great Procession' through London in support of imprisoned suffragettes who were on hunger strike. Note that the banner was carried by men supporting the women's cause.

The 1918 Act was passed near the end of World War I. As almost a million British men had been killed in the war, the Act was not greeted with public celebrations. Besides, winning the vote did not give women full equality with men. There was still a long way to go.

SECOND-CLASS CITIZENS

At the time of Emily Davison's death, the great majority of women received only basic schooling. Most of the better jobs were closed to them and they were paid less than men for the same work. The law gave women inadequate protection against abuse, too. Some men still regarded their wives as servants or, worse still, mere possessions. In short, women were second-class citizens.

Parliament

Equality

Women wanted to vote in parliamentary elections and sit in **Parliament** because they sought equality with men. Parliament was the most powerful institution in the land. The government operated through Parliament and all new laws were made there.

Women like Emily Davison argued that, to achieve equality with men, women first needed the vote and the right to become **MPs**, or Members of Parliament.

Parliament unreformed

The all-male Parliament consisted of an unelected **House of Lords** and a more powerful, elected **House of Commons**. During the 18th century, the election of MPs had been haphazard. Some deserted towns, like Old Sarum in Wiltshire, that had few if any inhabitants, still elected MPs, whilst growing industrial cities, like Birmingham and Manchester, had no MPs at all.

The House of Commons about ten years before the passing of the Reform Act, 1832. As all MPs were men, the Commons had the atmosphere (and customs) of a men's club. This did not change much until the very end of the 20th century.

The right to vote – the franchise – varied enormously. In some **constituencies** most adult men voted; in others only a handful of privileged men could do so. Surprisingly, in a few constituencies a handful of wealthy women had the franchise.

Reform

From the late 18th century, **radicals** like the MP John Wilkes demanded parliamentary reform. They wanted the House of Commons to represent more accurately the people it governed.

Eventually, in 1832, a Reform **Act** introduced some changes. It removed 'rotten **boroughs**' like Old Sarum. It also standardized the franchise, which was based on property (usually the ownership of land or a house). For women, this was a step backwards: from now on only a privileged group of 'male persons' had the vote. All women, even property owners, were excluded.

An anti-female Chartist cartoon in the political magazine *Punch,* 1848. It suggests that female Chartists should not be taken seriously and can be scared out of their radical views by rats, mice and cockroaches.

CHARTISM

In the later 1830s and 1840s the Chartist movement campaigned for universal male **suffrage**. Although Chartists did not call for female suffrage, women were active in its ranks:

'We have been told that the province of women is her home, and that the field of politics should be left to men; this we deny; the nature of things renders it impossible. … Is it not true that the interests of our fathers, husbands, and brothers, ought to be ours?'

'Address of the Female Political Union of Newcastle-upon-Tyne to their Fellow-country-women,' *Northern Star*, 9 February 1839.

The call for reform

Widening the male franchise

The 1832 Reform **Act** granted the vote to about one in five adult males. It limited the vote to those with property. Most **MPs** believed that because they had a 'stake' in the country, such people could be trusted to act responsibly. The Act reflected MPs' prejudice against working class and women. As no working-class men owned property, the Act made sure that they – like women – did not have the vote.

Radical thinkers, like the author and politician Tom Paine, said that the right to vote should not depend on property. Gradually, under pressure from groups like the Chartists, MPs realized that the parliamentary system would be strengthened if more 'responsible' people (such as middle-class men who had made money from industry) participated in it.

An 1860s cartoon mocking the women's rights movement. It shows John Bull (the cartoon representation of the traditional British male) blocking the door against a mob of unattractive spinsters. A pretty mother and her daughters (supposedly happy with their lot) look on scornfully.

AN "UGLY RUSH"!

MR. BULL: "Not if I know it!" *(See Division on the Woman's Vote Bill.)*

Please help us! Emily Davies (centre right) and Elizabeth Garrett Anderson (centre left) present a petition for greater female equality to the MP John Stuart Mill. Davies campaigned successfully for women to be allowed to take degrees at London University; Anderson was England's first qualified female doctor.

'ENTIRELY IRRELEVANT'

In his essay on 'Representative Government' (1861), the outstanding Victorian thinker John Stuart Mill argued that a person's sex was *'entirely irrelevant'* in politics: *'All human beings have the same interest in good government; the welfare of all is … affected by it, and they have equal need of a voice in it to secure their share of its benefits. If there be any difference, women require it more than men, since, being physically weaker, they are more dependent on law and society for protection.'*

Eventually the male franchise was extended and the **constituencies** re-arranged, in 1867 and again in 1884–5. Even so, before 1918 about 40 per cent of all adult males and all women still had no right to vote.

'Man' or 'Person'?

Inspired by Mary Wollstonecraft (see page 12) and others, in 1851 some Sheffield women founded a Women's Political Association to campaign for women's political rights. Their cause was taken up by the **Liberal** MP John Stuart Mill.

Mill tried to get the word 'man' changed to 'person' in the 1867 Reform **Bill**, so that some women could get the vote. His idea was rejected. Women responded by forming **suffrage** (voting rights) campaign groups in London, Birmingham, Bristol, Edinburgh and Manchester. Female suffrage was now an important political issue.

The weaker sex?

Bringers of evil

Both men and women put forward a variety of reasons – some rather strange – why women should not be **enfranchised**. Many Christians said their religion supported the supremacy of the male sex: its central figures – God and Jesus – were both masculine. Women were said to be psychologically weaker than men – the Bible even blamed a woman (Eve) for bringing evil into the world.

The traditional, respectable Victorian family, about 1845. The father, as the head of the family, reads from the Bible while his family kneel at prayer before him.

Mistress of the home

Traditionalists believed men and women had different purposes in life. Public activities like politics, business and war were men's jobs. Women were best suited to private duties, such as producing and raising children and running the home. If they dabbled in politics, they undermined their true calling.

Women were considered irrational, emotional and superficial, and therefore unsuited to the serious business of government. These arguments were circular: because women were considered irrational, they received little education; because they were uneducated in the affairs of government, they appeared irrational.

THE ANTI-SUFFRAGISTS

A wide range of people from all classes opposed female **suffrage** during the period 1880–1914. Among the more prominent were Florence Nightingale, and the Liberal Prime Minister William Gladstone. One celebrated doctor, Sir Almroth Wright, suggested women were too unstable to vote:

'… *upsettings of her mental equilibrium are the things that a women has most cause to fear; and no doctor can ever lose sight of the fact that the mind of a women is always threatened with danger from the reverberations of her physiological* [bodily] *emergencies.' The Times*, 28 March 1912.

A life of constant drudgery: women in a crowded slum in London's Golden Lane. Lack of birth control meant that most women spent their adult lives bringing up their large families. A family of ten children was not uncommon.

Strange creatures

The Victorians had their own anti-female prejudices. Women were a majority of the population. Many men feared that if women got the vote, they would control the political system to their benefit. **Liberals** and **socialists** thought women would always vote **Conservative**. **Imperialists** feared that women would use political power to promote birth control and so reduce the country's population. This would lead to a smaller army and navy to defend the British **Empire**. Finally, most **MPs** had been raised in the all-male world of boarding schools, Oxford and Cambridge universities and the armed forces. Many saw women as strange, remote, even threatening creatures.

Women's rights

Women's contribution

Supporters of votes for women frequently drew on the evidence of history. They pointed out that women had been able politicians (Queen Elizabeth I), mighty warriors (Boudicca), skilled writers (Jane Austen) and even successful pirates (Anne Bonny). As mentioned, some women had the vote before 1832. Female factory workers helped produce Britain's wealth and power. Moreover, the throne was occupied by a woman, Queen Victoria (although she opposed women's rights).

Limited lives

In the early 19th century women were not just denied the vote. They could not go to university or enter the professions, such as the law. Divorce was almost impossible while mothers who separated from their husbands lost **custody** of their children. Married women's property belonged to their husbands, and men were permitted to beat their wives.

The Women's Movement

Writers like Mary Wollstonecraft and Caroline Norton campaigned for more equal rights for women. Sympathetic male **MPs** supported some of the campaigners' demands, leading to legislation (laws) that increased women's rights. Separated women got custody of their children (1839, 1873), married women could keep their property (1870, 1882) and separation of married couples was simplified (1878, 1895). By 1913 there were women **graduates**, doctors, mayors, factory inspectors and **magistrates**.

Mary Wollstonecraft (1759–97), the **radical** campaigner for women's rights. Her equally famous daughter Mary was the author of the remarkable novel *Frankenstein*.

'ENLIGHTENING PRINCIPLES'

Mary Wollstonecraft's *Vindication of the Rights of Woman* (1792) was one of the earliest and most powerful arguments for women's rights. Equality in education, she argued, was essential:

'*... in order to spread those enlightening principles, which alone can ameliorate* [make better] *the fate of man, women must be allowed to found their virtue on knowledge. ... It is plain from the history of all nations, that women cannot be confined to merely domestic pursuits, for they will not fulfil family duties, unless their minds take a wider range. ... Nor can they be shut out of great enterprises. ...*'

However, women in these positions were exceptions. Paid employment for working-class women was limited to factory work, domestic service (as servants for the wealthy) and menial jobs, such as taking in washing. Most middle-class women were restricted to teaching, office work or acting as governesses. Female **suffrage** campaigners said this would change only when women were **enfranchised** and sat in **Parliament**.

These privileged pioneers are female undergraduates at work in the laboratory of Girton College, Cambridge, about 1910. In the early 19th century, the great majority of women had no secondary education, let alone the opportunity to take a degree.

Small steps forward

Local votes

Although women did not get the parliamentary vote until 1918, they did gain the vote in local elections. **MPs** imagined that local matters, being nearer the home, concerned women; whereas national matters, such as taxation and foreign affairs, did not.

In 1869 single women were permitted to vote in town council elections. The next year, they were able to vote for and sat on boards supervising local schools. Married women were not allowed to vote because it was believed they could be represented by their husbands!

Fears unfounded

From 1875, women became Poor Law Guardians (responsible for the poor in their district). This was important as male Guardians were often unsympathetic to destitute women. By 1907 women voted in most other local elections and were elected as local councillors.

The anxieties of those opposed to female **suffrage** (see pages 10-11) were not borne out by the impact of women voters – government did not collapse and women did not vote for silly or illogical laws. Moreover, women worked as well as men in local government. This undermined arguments against giving them the parliamentary vote.

Women of the Match Makers' Union whom Annie Besant led into a successful strike for better pay in 1888. The strike had a considerable impact on public opinion and showed women what they could achieve through collective action.

A GREAT CAMPAIGNER

Annie Besant (1847–1933) was at the forefront of the Victorian campaign for equal rights for women. After separating from her clergyman husband and losing **custody** of her daughter, she called for divorce reform. In 1877 she was prosecuted for publishing one of Britain's first birth control handbooks (*The Fruits of Philosophy*). In 1888, now a **socialist**, she organized a strike by badly paid women working in the match-making industry. In the same year she was elected to the London School Board.

Women in politics

Meanwhile, more women were getting involved in national politics because the main political parties needed women's help to access the growing **electorate**.

The **Liberals** and recently formed **Labour** Party founded women's sections. Women dominated the Primrose League, a political society which promoted **Conservative** values. By 1913 all parties relied on female party workers to run local organizations, **canvass** the electorate and even speak at public meetings. Nevertheless, such work was largely limited to middle-class women. Most working-class women – tired, under-educated and poorly paid – had neither the time nor the energy to participate actively in politics.

The outcasts? This suffragette poster of about 1900 pointed out that, like criminals and lunatics, a female **graduate** had no right to vote in parliamentary elections.

The campaign grows

The moderates

By 1872 regional women's **suffrage** societies had united into the Central Committee for Women's Suffrage. In 1897 this became the National Union of Women's Suffrage Societies (NUWSS).

Led first by Lydia Becker and later by Millicent Fawcett, the NUWSS's 'suffragists' used moderate tactics. They campaigned by writing books and pamphlets, holding peaceful meetings and supporting **MPs** who backed their cause.

The suffragists wanted the vote on the same terms as men. That is, that women with property should have the vote. Between 1870 and 1900, MPs frequently introduced **bills** to this effect. Had they become law, married women whose property (their home) was in their husband's name, would not have been **enfranchised**.

The voice of moderation. Millicent Fawcett of the suffragist NUWSS addressing a meeting in Hyde Park, London, about 1913. The membership of the NUWSS grew rapidly when the WSPU suffragettes were at their most violent.

The militants

The suffrage movement divided the political parties. For instance, **Labour's** first MP Keir Hardie, supported it. Other Labour leaders rejected it, seeking instead the vote for all adults, irrespective of whether they were male or female.

In 1903, fed up with the suffragists' lack of progress, Emmeline Pankhurst and her daughters Christabel and Sylvia formed the Women's Social and Political Union (WSPU).

THE PANKHURSTS

The Manchester born **radical** Emmeline Pankhurst and her daughter Christabel (who had been prevented from training as a barrister because of her sex) believed the WSPU would succeed only if it remained a largely middle-class movement. This caused a family rift with Emmeline's other daughter, Sylvia, who believed the WSPU should be a **socialist** organization campaigning for the rights of working-class women. Emmeline, Christabel and Sylvia were arrested several times for their militant tactics.

Members of the WSPU were given the title of 'suffragettes' to distinguish them from the more moderate 'suffragists' of the NUWSS. The WSPU's 'suffragettes' pledged to attack the government, of whatever party, and force it to grant women's suffrage. Their tactics included mass rallies and vivid posters.

By 1909, the suffragettes had moved on to stone throwing and other violent acts. Most newspapers, although broadly sympathetic towards the women's cause, were hostile to suffragette violence.

Emmeline (left) and Christabel Pankhurst in prison clothing after being sentenced for lawless behaviour. The suffragettes' violent acts, such as smashing windows, certainly drew attention to their cause. However, it may also have set it back by offending less radical supporters of female rights.

Stalemate

Crisis years

In the years 1909–14 Britain was very unsettled because of strikes, tensions between the European powers and the violence of the suffragettes. Also the **Liberal** government clashed with the **House of Lords** when it broke with tradition by rejecting the 1909 budget, forcing two general elections in 1910.

Suffragettes

The Prime Minister Henry Asquith refused to discuss the issue of women's **suffrage** with the WSPU and out of frustration suffragettes turned to more violent tactics such as window smashing. For these acts several went to prison. In 1910, the WSPU called a truce, reverting to peaceful protest while **Parliament** discussed various women's suffrage measures.

Sylvia Pankhurst, whose Women's Social Defence League carried the campaign for women's rights to the working-class women of London's East End. She is speaking to a crowd in Bow Road, East London, in October 1912.

When these failed, the WSPU was furious and militancy rose to new heights. Suffragettes set fire to mail boxes and even fire bombed churches and private houses. Imprisoned suffragettes went on hunger strike, refusing all food in the hope this would draw attention to their cause. The government responded with a 'Cat and Mouse' **Act** (see box). This did little to curb the violent protest, Emily Davison's tragic death occurring two months after the Act was passed (see page 4).

Suffragists

The suffragettes kept women's suffrage in the news. Surprisingly, dislike of their tactics increased the popularity of the moderate NUWSS. By 1914 its membership – the 'suffragists' – had risen from 12,000 to over 50,000, including many working-class women.

Meanwhile, **Labour's** attitude towards the NUWSS had softened. The Union responded by supporting Labour **candidates**. This alarmed the Liberal government, which feared the growing strength of the Labour movement. Therefore when war broke out in 1914, for a number of reasons government ministers were already talking of settling the female suffrage issue once and for all.

Chasing the sympathy vote, 1909. This suffragette poster appeals to male voters to reject the Liberal government because of its policy of force-feeding suffragette prisoners who are on hunger strike.

THE CAT AND MOUSE ACT, 1913

After 1909 imprisoned suffragettes went on hunger strike for the right to be treated as political prisoners, not criminals. Forced feeding of prisoners, many from 'respectable' middle-class backgrounds, caused a public outcry. In response, the government passed a law (nicknamed the 'Cat and Mouse' Act) that allowed prisoners to be set free until their health was restored, then re-arrested. Sylvia Pankhurst was arrested and released thirteen times.

War and victory

Immediate effect of war

The outbreak of World War I in August 1914 brought the **suffrage** campaigns to an abrupt halt. Women realized that the country had more urgent issues to attend to. The NUWSS stopped its activities. When suffragette prisoners were released, the WSPU called a truce. Emmeline Pankhurst switched her energies to recruiting soldiers – men, not women.

Women at work

With millions of men fighting in France, the country faced a serious labour shortage. The problem was solved by recruiting women workers. Many worked in factories, especially making weapons. Others did work never previously done by women, such as driving buses and lorries.

Although the government and the press loudly praised women's help with the war effort, the

Women working in an engineering shop during World War I. Although women proved as skilful as men in this type of work, their jobs were given back to male soldiers returning from the front after the war.

improvement in women's employment opportunities did not last (see page 23). Nevertheless, women's invaluable contribution helped win over those who had previously doubted their strength and steadfastness. To some extent, therefore, the granting of the parliamentary vote to women in 1918 was a 'reward' for the remarkable way they had served the nation between 1914 and 1918.

The vote

In 1916 the government set up a conference to determine how the next election should be organized. The conference decided that virtually all men over 21 and women (including wives) over the age of 30 should be **enfranchised**. The higher age qualification for women was to prevent men being outnumbered. This decision became law in the 1918 Representation of the People **Act**, which passed the **House of Commons** by 387 votes to 57.

At last! Women electors casting their votes in the general election of December 1918. Only women over the age of 30 were permitted to vote. Not until the end of the century were substantial numbers of women elected to the House of Commons.

THE FIRST WOMEN MPS

The 1918 Representation of the People Act was quickly followed by an Act allowing women to sit as **MPs**. Of the seventeen women **candidates**, only one – Countess Constance Markiewicz – was elected (for a Dublin **constituency**). At the time she was in prison on suspicion of anti-British activities, and did not take her seat. The next year American-born Lady Nancy Astor was elected for a Plymouth constituency in a by-election and so became the first woman MP to sit in the House of Commons.

The impact of women

Lady Nancy Astor, Britain's first female MP, standing between prime minister David Lloyd George (right) and former prime minister Arthur Balfour. Astor described her first six months in the House of Commons as 'sheer hell'.

Equal terms at last

After 1918 about 42 per cent of the **electorate** were women. However, only a tiny percentage of parliamentary **candidates** were women: only four per cent (69) in 1929. Of these, just fourteen were elected to the **House of Commons** out of a total of 615 **MPs**.

The handful of women MPs were able and respected and women voters divided between the parties much as men did. The exception was the 1923 election, when many women rejected **Conservative** policies that threatened to increase food prices.

As a result, hardly anyone objected when, in 1928, the franchise was given to women over the age of 21 on the same terms as men.

Slow advance

The campaign for female **suffrage** was part of the broader movement for equal rights for women. But those who hoped for a swift advance to full equality were disappointed.

Parliament did pass some new measures that helped women. These included laws in 1923 and 1937 that made divorce easier, the introduction of widows' pensions in 1925 and the crucial Family Allowance **Act** of 1945. This arranged for government money to be paid directly to mothers, so that irresponsible fathers could not keep it for themselves.

Real help for mothers and their children: a woman collects her first weekly family allowance of 5 shillings (25p) per child, August 1946.

Not yet equal

Although 1918 marked a significant gain in women's political rights, they were still discriminated against in many other areas. The Pre-War Practices Act of 1919, for example, reserved many jobs for those who had done them before the war. This had the effect of excluding women from the new (and often better paid) areas of employment they had entered during the war. For many years thereafter, the political parties largely ignored other important women's issues, such as birth control and equal pay.

WOMEN EXCLUDED

In 1920 the feminist campaigner Eleanor Rathbone was scathing in her criticism of the Pre-War Practices Act of 1919:

'One of the first fruits of the first parliament elected partly by women has been this … Act which, without mentioning the word 'woman' or 'female', has the effect of legally excluding women from nearly every department of skilled industry except a few trades traditionally their own'.

Reflecting the nation?

Slow to change

Throughout the 20th century women were not well represented in **Parliament**, even though they were the majority of the **electorate**. This was partly because political parties did not encourage women to become **candidates**.

For the 1931 election, for example, 62 candidates (4.8 per cent) and 15 **MPs** (2.4 per cent) were women. This had hardly changed by 1970, when 5.4 per cent of the candidates and 4.1 per cent of MPs (26 out of 630) were women.

A 'gentlemen's club'

The handful of women MPs (only 240 in total between 1918 and 2000) meant Parliament remained a type of 'gentlemen's club'. The hours it kept – sometimes sitting late into the night – made life difficult for women who were still expected to look after their young children. The refusal to change such arrangements indicated that the majority of MPs believed that married women with children should be at home, not in Parliament.

The fight goes on! Women MPs (left to right) Irene Ward, Barbara Castle and Edith Summerskill with a petition demanding equal pay for women, March 1954. Although an Equal Pay **Act** came into force 21 years later, wage discrimination remained for many more years in isolated industries.

Nevertheless, women MPs made their mark. In 1924, Margaret Bondfield became the first woman to join the government. Five years later, as Minister for Labour, she was the first female **cabinet** member. By 1970 **backbench** women MPs had brought in 26 new laws on matters such as nursing homes and selling alcohol to children. This showed women MPs being more sensitive than their male colleagues to the needs of the female population.

Behind the times

Parliament was slow to reflect the changing mood of the nation, just as it had been over the question of female **suffrage**. By 1966 over five million married women were in work, compared with under one million in 1930. Yet Parliament had still done nothing about equal pay.

Low qualifications, low expectations, low pay. Female workers in the Champion spark plug factory, 1957. For most of the 20th century the majority of women left school with few qualifications. They were not expected to have careers and so were therefore limited to dull, poorly-paid jobs.

The women's movement

Women's liberation

During the 1960s, a 'Women's Liberation Movement' took root in Britain. Two important social changes lay behind it: firstly, effective contraception, especially the birth-control pill, which gave women more control over their lives; and secondly, the growing number of women in full- or part-time employment. This meant they had their own money and were not dependent on the earnings of their male partners.

Picking up the new mood, **Parliament** passed laws that allowed abortion for social reasons (as opposed to just medical ones) and divorce when a marriage had broken down.

Equal opportunities

Finally, in the 1970s, Parliament introduced the **radical** changes to the law that many women had been seeking. These included equal pension rights, paid maternity leave, and, at last, an Equal Pay **Act** (1970) to come into force by 1975. The Sex Discrimination Act (1975) set up an Equal Opportunities

The number of female MPs remained disappointingly low until the 1990s. Nevertheless, women were increasingly willing to express their political views in non-parliamentary ways. These protestors are objecting to the arrival of US nuclear cruise missiles at Greenham Common air base in 1982.

Commission to monitor discrimination in areas such as employment, education and housing.

Helped by the Commission, more women were able to lead fuller, more varied and rewarding lives. They were better able to make their mark in areas where men had dominated, such as the law, business and even the armed forces.

A changing Parliament

As before, Parliament itself was slow to change. Despite the success of Margaret Thatcher, the first woman prime minister (1979–90), the 120 women **MPs** elected in 1997 still found the **House of Commons**' rules, customs and facilities geared towards male MPs. Nevertheless, Parliament has recently seen a woman **speaker** (Betty Boothroyd, 1992–2000), the creation of the post of Minister for Women and several women in the **cabinet**. Thus in the 21st century the House of Commons and government is beginning, albeit slowly, to lose its traditional all-male image and atmosphere.

MARGARET THATCHER

Benefiting from the pioneering work of earlier feminists, Margaret Thatcher went to Oxford University and then trained as a lawyer before becoming a **Conservative** MP in 1959. She was elected leader of her party in 1975 and became Britain's first woman prime minister in 1979. During her long and controversial premiership, however, members of the women's movement criticized her for not doing more to help their cause.

The slow march

Why so long?

Sixty-one years elapsed between John Stuart Mill's attempt to get women the franchise on the same terms as men and the final victory in 1928. One reason why it took so long was that centuries of prejudice had to be overcome. Attitudes did not change overnight.

A second reason was practical: although many agreed with the principle of giving some women the vote, they disagreed over which women. This was especially so before 1918, when not all men were **enfranchised**. A third reason was fear: political parties were worried that female voters would change the political system in ways they could not foretell.

Only the beginning

As we have seen, female **suffrage** did not mean equal rights. Another 47 years elapsed between winning the franchise and the 1975 Sex Discrimination **Act**.

Staff and pupils of a local girls' school, 1890. At this time only a small proportion of middle-class women thought of education as the key to a career outside their traditional role as mothers and housewives.

100 YEARS ON

Writing in the 1880s, Annie Besant believed women's liberation was close at hand: *'The chains bound round her [woman] … are being broken … and soon she shall walk upright and unfettered in the sunshine, the friend, the helper, the lover, but never more the slave, of man.' Woman's Position According to the Bible,* 1885.

Writing almost a century later, Rosalind Miles warned that the struggle for full equality was far from over: *'Nowhere do women enjoy the rights, privileges and possibilities and leisure time that men do. Everywhere men still mediate between women and power, women and the state, women and freedom, women and themselves.' The Women's History of the World,* 1988.

Role reversal. Girls of the Rainham Mark Grammar School receive their excellent A level results, 1996. By the end of the 20th century girls were outstripping boys in all areas of secondary education: a complete reversal of the situation in Emily Davison's day.

Moreover, the effect of the Act took years to filter through into everyday life. Even in the early 21st century, **Parliament** remained a largely male institution.

Emily's legacy

The development of equal rights for women is marked with significant moments rather than profound turning points. Emily Davison's death was one such moment. It showed just how passionately some women felt about their cause. Whatever people felt about women's rights, after Derby Day 1913 it was a cause they could not ignore.

Time-line

1792 Mary Wollstonecraft publishes *Vindication of the Rights of Woman*

1832 Great Reform Act reforms the old electorate and constituency system. Women deprived of the vote.

1857 For the first time divorce possible without an Act of Parliament

1867 Parliament rejects John Stuart Mill's suggestion that women be given the vote on the same terms as men. Second Reform Act extends the male franchise.

1869 Women gain the vote in town council elections

1870 Married Women's Property Act allows married women to retain some of their own earnings

1872 Central Committee for Women's Suffrage founded

1875 Women permitted to become Poor Law Guardians

1884 Third Reform Act extends the male franchise

1897 National Union of Women's Suffrage Societies (NUWSS) founded

1903 Women's Social and Political Union (WSPU) founded by women disappointed by the moderate tactics of the NUWSS

1905 First suffragettes imprisoned for disrupting a Liberal rally

1908 Around 50,000 attend a women's suffrage rally in Hyde Park

1909 Imprisoned suffragettes go on hunger strike

1910 Suffragettes call a truce while women's suffrage is debated in the House of Commons (to 1912)

1911–3 Suffragettes begin campaign of window smashing and arson – setting fire to mail boxes and buildings

1913 Cat and Mouse Act. Suffragette Emily Davison killed when she falls under the king's horse during the Derby.

1914 Outbreak of World War I; women's suffrage societies suspend their activities

1918 Representation of the People Act gives the vote to women over the age of 30

1919 Nancy Astor becomes the first women MP to take her seat in the House of Commons. Pre-war Practices Act denies women the opportunity to take many jobs in manufacturing.

1924 Margaret Bondfield becomes the first woman MP to join the government

1928 Representation of the People Act gives the vote to women on the same terms as men

1929 Margaret Bondfield becomes the first woman MP to join the cabinet

1945 Family Allowance Act – came into force in 1946

1969 Divorce Reform Act – breakdown of marriage accepted as grounds for divorce

1970 Equal Pay Act – came into force in 1975

1975 Sex Discrimination Act

1979 Margaret Thatcher becomes the first woman prime minister (to 1990)

1997 120 women MPs elected, doubling the number of women MPs